Listening to the Night

Listening to the Night
Jane Routh

smith|doorstop

Published 2018 by
Smith|Doorstop books
The Poetry Business
Campo House
54 Campo Lane
Sheffield S1 2EG
www.poetrybusiness.co.uk

ISBN 978-1-912196-17-3

British Library Cataloguing-in-Publication Data.
A catalogue record for this book is available from the
British Library.

Designed & Typeset by Utter
Printed and bound by CPI Group (UK) Ltd, Croydon, CR0 4YY
Author photo: Mike Barlow

Smith|Doorstop Books are represented by and members
of Inpress, www.inpressbooks.co.uk. Distributed by NBN
International, Airport Business Centre, 10 Thornbury Road
Plymouth PL 6 7PP.

The Poetry Business receives financial support from
Arts Council England

Supported by
ARTS COUNCIL
ENGLAND

Contents

for Mike

Lately, I've taken to listening to the night

There are many darknesses. Moonlit ones are no good:
your eyes interfere, re-invent what you know.
True dark (the stone barn indistinguishable
against night skies) brings word from away:

the shape of the valley downstream as a gust powers up,
tyres on wet tarmac. Once, a train. A train!
I remember reading how cold air curves sound waves
towards earth. Still nights are the widest.

When the owls call, I follow high into the night
until they hunt – the kill is soundless.
An hour before dawn, they beat their bounds.
I echo the one who lives close, but no reply –

just cold air on bare skin at the flung-open sash
as river-rush pours in, falling over itself
in its urge for the sea, constant
as the bypass town-dwellers tell you they don't hear.

3am

What if you listen and there's nothing,
not even the unheard tick of the alarm
you shushed on the bathroom shelf,
not even the hum/not-hum of the fridge.
What if you open the window
and the world out there holds its breath
then steals about its business in secret,
every droplet in the river sliding seawards
in silence. You'd be left with half phrases
from those seventies LPs you listened to last week
Wish I had a river, or a memory that replays
in an endless loop where the phone rings
Sorry your call cannot be taken at the moment
and an old man pushes up from his chair, balances
then picks up and says *O yes it can*,
every time, his little triumph over the machine –
you'd want them all back: the force eight
blasting down from the north with hail
then a cloudburst, you'd want
sheep bleating for their auctioned lambs,
muckspreaders, hedge-flails, alarmist pheasants,
even that kid on the nightshift moped
who woke you a couple of hours ago
changing down and revving the length of the valley
until you could tell exactly which bend he'd take next.
Yes, you'd want the whole rackety mess of it
to keep you from listening to yourself
and the background thunder of your blood.

My neighbour killed on the road

Afterwards – when I knew what had happened –
I remembered waking in the early hours,
his wife's voice: *Wik?* she was calling, *Wik?*

Even half-asleep, it was unsettling:
she'd always been the silent type
keeping herself to herself and her tabs on him –

he was the talker. You'd hear him fields away
grumbling to himself, unmistakeable
that stutter at the end of his sentence.

He was always on the lookout, knew
where everyone was in the valley,
kept up a running commentary, missed nothing

which makes you wonder how it could have happened –
below a blind bend, yes, but with hearing like his
he'd have known a vehicle was coming.

Strange how much I miss him, how
the air in the valley, long nights and
arriving home all feel shapeless now;

strange how I listen for him – almost call out *Wik?* myself –
as if I'd never driven over the mess on the road,
threads of grey feather pressed into tarmac.

Sometimes I drive home over Mealbank

I forgot to look at my watch:
a gate-on-wheels blocks the lane.
I switch off. Time slows.
Fine drizzle drifts over the hedge.
A long wait. A cow comes
down the lane towards the car,
hopskips left into the yard.
The first one? or last? Two more
up into the yard, four, then a laneful
crowding down towards the gate,
lifting their heads over the top bar,
more heads shouldering through
for a mournful stare at the car,
one head that can't get through settling
for a tongue's-worth of hedge –
garlic mustard, vetches and brome
– and the collie weaving between
hind legs shifting a few, but still
more eye-pools of black melancholy
over the gate, considering;
a flick of the wiper switch ripples
a shock of alarm through the herd
so legs pick their way to the parlour
as if balanced on tight high-heels
and still they keep coming, all different,
one plain white with a single black hock,
the collie in charge now as they thin
to small groups, a last half-dozen
in front of the quad bike. I wait.

Time passes. A last old lady turns
into the lane and limps along, rests
her bad leg, limps, rests and makes it.
I wait. The gate's wheeled away,
a wave; I smile. Nothing
remarkable, only this pause

On the flightpath to Ireland

Something about shortening day lengths
like clockwork under these endless clear skies;
something about the dryness, the strange lack of wind
and no frosts, that matters too, but this year the leaves –
this year the ash have held on, their dull leaves
brightening to lime, to lemon (the kitchen
seasoned with their yellow glow)
as their crowns bleach each day lighter and lighter
until they're so airy and buoyant
they must slowly lift off like helium balloons
to drift over the valley – but no, look, all at once
the air's studded with fieldfares from Scandinavia
none of their usual intent and direction,
some turning back east, others stalling, treading air,
the whole flock milling in confusion
as if – in spite of its shelter, berries and haws –
this vivid landscape triggers alarms,
their species flightplan insisting on dour,
on refuelling at a steep wooded valley, grey
with bare-branched ash – so they're off again westwards,
off as fast as the leaves will be
next time so much as a birdweight knocks a branch.

Elegy for a book

Hedges, *Collins New Naturalist Library NN58, 1974; cover
Clifford & Rosemary Ellis*

Hard to find. And more so after a six-page spread
in a colour supplement – so the surprise of it, cover
bright spring green with a curve in a dove-grey road.
That light touch of the Ellis's: sponged cow-parsley heads
and one orange-tip leading your eye
to distances beyond hedges chalky with may

– of its time but unfaded: no marks, no stains
only a red sticker on the flyleaf FOR REFERENCE ONLY,
West Glamorgan County Library paying £4.50
in 1978, and you paying even less,
forgetting how much time has passed since then
and shocked to find your own past already

history: you'd planted the first hedge of your own
back then, when a man in a tweed jacket
stood on a cart manhandling a rotary saw
to chop back a hedge top. Which of elm or thorn hedges
linnets or buntings prefer, now of no odds:
all those miles of surveyed hedgerows lost.

How long is a hedge? As long as will stock-proof
a field. How big is a field? As much as a two-horse team
can plough in a day. How old is a hedge? A century a species
in thirty paces – the formula and its caveats, the welter of facts
you thought you needed to know, adding
to the fools' gold weight of nostalgia you hoard.

The blackberries

So clean and sweet, we stood there eating
at the woodland edge above the glen
– its ruined houses here and there along the burn
but clustered closer to the crag than I'd expected –
and realised, if she had left along this track,
here is where she would have turned
to take the last look at the place; this is where
she would have seen *the houses already being stripped*
– though she speaks this in another language
a minister writes down and forty years will pass
before his son translates the pain of her eviction
as *the hissing of the fire on the hearthstone of the house,*
when they drowned it, reached my heart –
yet hers is not my history to lay claim to:
our paths cross only at some brambles whose fruit
she could have tasted two centuries before
– you know how their long stems splay out
bending to fresh ground, tips rooting down, taking hold,
new growth the same and not the same.

English evictions may have been more subtle,
though starvation no less effective than crowbars
at driving from the village they were born in
the family of my grandfather's grandfather,
agricultural labourers walking to the coast,
shoemakers when they arrived. Some shipped out,
a scattering, the usual.
                                    But on my mother's side,
Swing Rioters: they were having none of it,
unlawfully, maliciously and feloniously
damaging a threshing machine. Taken into custody

and tried at the assizes, next stop should have been
Van Diemen's Land – yet not: too lame, too weak
to bother with. And what's to be done on poor relief
but send your son away north for railway work,
knowing your first goodbye will be your last
as you watch him walk towards the bend in the lane,
where he stops, makes as if to gather a handful of berries
then turns   waves.

Why there is nothing

A glass case in the centre of the floor
displays plaster potatoes painted with blight;
a worn piece of tree root is offered

that may (or may not) have been used
as a three-legged stool to sit by a hearth
which was cold, stone-cold.

*They used to knock the houses all-together
and they used this tool for that purpose.*
A crowbar hangs on the wall.

Nothing is left for the Famine Museum
because there was nothing to leave
after houses were razed and lives erased.

My mother had nothing of her own mother's
for remembrance – even the single photograph
on her glass-topped dressing table, a modern copy.

It had always seemed strange to me:
her family was poor, yet gardeners
were always in work. My mother

couldn't really explain. She supposed
she was young, must have wanted modern
things, not old stuff from *home*.

※

And how little I kept of hers. She'd long replaced
furniture my father made (the front parlour
his workshop) with Reproduction.

I'd enough of my own, no need
of a dinner-service bought one piece at a time
kept for best in the false roof

and couldn't face worldy goods house-clearance men
packed as if in a speeded-up film, too fast
to say *maybe, you never know* ... What's left

for the Museum of Setting up Home in the War?
Here, I could say, here's a ring of 1940's gold:
look how thin it is. How worn.

Holy detritus

They couldn't explain how it happened,
workmen clearing the basement at Rydal:
one minute they carried her between them,
next, she was across the floor

her bare feet, habit, book, hands, quill
smashed to plaster-fragment and paint-chip,
almost as if she'd leapt from their hold
they told each other, watching her head roll away

intact – even her nose – over the flagstones,
like the shell of a thrush egg you found
on the pavement under the lilac and turned
so its black-speckled shapeliness appeared

whole and as if still filled by mysterious life.
Nervous of Teresa's head, Teresa
with her ecstasies and not-quite smile
– the saint of headaches – they left it in the church

where its whys and hows will be forgotten
– along with those of the box pew, an oak cupboard,
two seventeenth century pew ends stacked at the back,
and all those bones and stones.

Earthmover

He cleared the desert, drew a line across it to true north and stood three hundred giant boulders along its length. At its centre, he scooped out an amphitheatre for five thousand, its stage an eye with an eyelash lagoon glinting sky. By way of distance and backdrop, he sculpted a line of cliffs like Wastwater Screes with a scalloped top.

He piled two cones of earth, sharp-edged and precise, each forty cubits high on a base a hundred cubits across: rivals to the great Mote of Urr. Crowned them with standing stones.

When I saw him he'd spent the morning at caterpillar pace hauling a huge slab to seal the Omphalos. He looked so young, sprawled full-length in the sun: gold earrings, Roman emperor pose – except instead of grapes his left hand held a Pepsi can. He was nearly done: roused himself and clanged the wide bucket off, hooked on the small one, swung the boom round and delicately inched that last slab into place, shovelled gravel on the gaps and battered it home.

Any day now – not a word to his mates – he'll be back to the usual: foundations, roads, sewers.

The Stone

And then there was the artist who told us
he'd carried a stone from the hill he could see
from his kitchen, shaped and polished it and put it back.
He'd marked the place; returned it transformed.

Its twin shone on his table, neither black nor red,
heavy, but just liftable, curves
electrified into life by their smoothness.
It seemed to hum. I thought it might move.

He wrote out co-ordinates for the wild stone
and we went looking, rough underfoot; climbed,
lined up bearings, quartered the ground,
reversed direction, but never found it.

Doubt crept in: could a work so beautiful
be abandoned among those rocks? If it didn't exist –
it does now, in the mind: a perfect dark shape
humming to its lost companion

(which went to London and was sold).

Hut of the shadows
after Chris Drury, Loch nam Madadh, 1997

Sheep pushed in, sheltering,
so someone fixed a wicket across the entrance.
Before that, head down against the wind
you could've passed it by, unknowing:

built from the rock on which it stood
and roofed with turf from round about, it seemed
merely a narrow passage into the earth,
(though one disorienting in its curve

until hands along the walls find a widening space
and a ledge to sit on in the dark.) How long
does it take for eyes to adjust? Stare
at the blackness, and the swimmy wall

will resolve into rushing wavelets on the loch,
and then it's sudden: blue water, grey islands,
hills and fast clouds flickering over the stones
like an old film of the world you have left

viewed from the afterlife. No, don't feel
for the lens the artist set in the wall at your back;
watch the wind write its passage on the shadows,
let it blow away the tender longing they induce:

the hut's not yet fallen back to its foundations
with future archaeologists shaking their heads,
reckoning it could have been a store – like the cleits
on St. Kilda – a different design, but certainly a store.

There is a place

where the cuckoo still calls until the light fades
in the cool green of the evening woods

where last year's barley stubble's studded through
with field pansy, daisy and storksbill

where larks still pin a cascade of notes to the sky
plummet earthwards and disappear into silence

and a burial ground you cannot tread for primroses
centuries of dead set just as thickly underneath

though it's a strange twenty-first century sort of joy
to feel, foundered between memory and desire –

for the barley's only cut late the old-fashioned way
on a grant and the skylarks have found a reserve

Bombus distinguendus

I remember the wind and a sift of fine white sand-grains stinging along the surface of dune and beach. It would have been autumn but I can't now say which island – North Uist? Berneray?

I remember the way the wind wrenched the car door from your hand, how hard it was to close, how calm inside the car and how a bee blew in with us – yellow-furred, a huge bee we couldn't dislodge from the dark crevice between windscreen and dash no matter how we flapped with our gloves and our maps. We had to let the wind scour the car.

A friend who lived nearby told us it was a rarity: all her life there and she'd not seen one – though years will pass before I look it up, to know it as a first-year daughter queen searching out some warm dry place to hibernate before her brief summer fling among the machair flowers.

I remember the wind. I remember the bee and my ignorance; I like to remember that.

Vernal equinox / partial eclipse

Everything as expected:
the morning trills of small birds petering out,
wind dropping and a chill setting in.

Thin cloud
              drifting apart
to ghost the sun with cirrus,
pale as the last sliver of a waning moon.

(I remember the last time as darker:
this is not even owl-light, it's rain-light:
I can smell it and my collar's up.)

The waiting's too much for the woodpecker.
He seizes the 9:33 moment, loud in the silence,
and hammers a drum roll, four times.

A flock of tits on the move. Farm dogs across the valley,
geese cackling. A breeze
and the full clear glory of a curlew from Perry Moor again and again,

light lifting fast now and the cloud not dark at all
but thinning again to cast the sun in a first-quarter-moon shape
9:45 it says on my scrap-paper sketches

– the sort of thing you just fold and pocket,
a surprise like an old concert ticket years later
grubby and worn: *Oh, look at this.*

Chambermaids Lizzie King
and Nellie Collinson see a new moon

I like that it happened in Scarborough: let's say
that it's evening and they're turning down beds.
Early May. They throw up a sash and lean out –
that clean smell off the sea. It's 1916: astronomy's
not on their minds, gazing out at the sea and clear sky.
Look, Lizzie, just there: can you see what I see? – glad
their first glimpse of the moon wasn't through glass.

So how did it get into the records,
their fourteen-and-half-hour-old moon?
Maybe a guest walks in as Nellie is pointing it out,
an old man who checks his almanac, disbelieving
their eyes could see a moon that young. Though I'd rather
Nellie come from a family of fishermen who read skies
as readily as that fictitious guest his book:

let her run and tell the harbourmaster. She knew
she'd sighted that moon early – as I did not
when I saw the thinnest curving thread of light last year.
What was it I saw not knowing, then, how it counted –
a thirty-hour moon? a forty-hour moon? I don't
remember the date, don't even remember the month.
A fine gold wire: I'm sure of the thing itself.

The Lack
for Elizabeth

If you could have sat with him
as he lay dying three hundred years ago
while cool evening air carried garden scents
through the open casement, and told him
they've discovered an enzyme they call
RhNUDX1, what would have astonished him
was not that it exists – for wasn't it self-evident,
his whole life spent working with it,
his dreams filled with it swelling and fading
and always something in it just beyond reach –
no, he would only have doubted you when you said
it was *missing*, perhaps could even be *bred back in*,
because how could it have been lost
when he, when all the old breeders, knew
that was the heart of it: arms filled
with his labours, he'd only to lift the latch
and his daughter would run to him
and dip her head to his hands, breathing
– her eyes closed – and then a second breath,
deeper, as if to fill her whole body and drown
in the perfume of it – the same gesture
his wife, God rest her soul, used to make
and even his patron Monsieur le Comte
would shut his eyes on the second deep breath
and forget the instructions he was giving
for his banquet, waving his courtiers away
as he turned to the rose garden, talking
of nothing but how it must be planted
to best effect, near a path, by the trellis, for this
ah, this one was indeed the essence of rose.
And if you'd tried to explain that new roses
bred for single buds and straight stalks

would lack scent, *No*, he would have said,
his thin frame racked by rare laughter, knowing
everyone always comes to a rose for its scent
– that first, and above all else – just as you did,
Elizabeth, bending to the old roses I'm growing
and breathing in the eyes-closed power of them
even when you needed my arm for support.

A garden bench

When I say *iron and rust*
it's to speak of loss and endurance:

it had belonged to my oldest aunt,
the one born in 1893,

and it stood by ramshackle wooden garages
she rented out for her widow's mite.

Of course not, I'd said, asked
if I wanted it when she died.

My father took it in hand. I remember
he said it took weeks to chisel off

the years of her doggedness – a coat
every spring, green paint or brown leftover

from the back scullery where you'd set down
the full pails you'd fetched from spring-wells

– and how surprised he was in the end
to find its iron wasn't plain circles, flat curves

but roses, and vines.
He painted it white.

Now it's here, paint crazed and metal
showing through, too heavy to dispose of,

too unwieldy, too long:
a weight two men struggle to lift.

When I say it falls to me now to fettle it
I mean memory of course,

chipping at layers flaking away,
replacing the slats and burnishing rust –

as if I could work back to some cast iron core
for painting black.

The moor road

The years of my father's loneliness,
I came to love the road over the moor,
its emptiness after the A65: *nearly home*
– though I loved it for itself as well,
the grey-blues and purples of its distances,
shine on the dry ochre grasses of winter
and, once, a white underwing flash in sunlight
that stopped me: a ghost owl beat out
from the heath and slowly carried away
some small dark death to a roofless barn
– but in all those journeys, nothing like this,
the air sharp after rain and a wavering brilliance
in the empty cleft of the furthest hills
shaping itself into the whiteness of a giant turbine,
fading, then re-forming, a whole choir of them now –
and for all that I can talk about refraction
and atmospheric ducting, no whit less marvellous
than the silvery city with its spires
which the citizens of Buffalo flocked to view
slowly rise up from Lake Ontario
one nineteenth century August morning,
thousands of them crowding on rooftops, marvelling
and some of them saying *a heavenly vision*
as a side-wheel steamer put into the shining bay.

She thinks she sees the swallows leave Cairn Holy

Her back to the *Interpretation Board*,
she re-forests the hills. The stones are
lovely: tall and slim and leaning
on the edge of eloquence, purpose
self-evident to their builders,
but gone.

The air's electric with swallows
– not feeding: these are fast, urgent
with their *spleee-plink* and aerobatics.
A pair plummets straight down
in front of her. She's no more to them
than stone.

Then silence; orphaned air. It's late afternoon:
the swallows are off, skittering sunwards –
hundreds of them, haphazard and zigzag.
She thought there'd be more southing
to their track. Things are never what
you expect.

How can she know whether
she's watching them leave? How
can you know when you wind down
a car window to wave goodbye
and shout *See you soon*,
you won't?

Untitled poem

Eyes on the stainless blade
one millimetre from finger ends,
white crescents with their mottled rind
falling in rows, yet the pile of orange fruits
seeming never to shrink; your mind away
at the end of its kite string –
that's why there are so many poems
about marmalade. This isn't another,
it's about grief: there was only
his one last winter my father didn't set to.

Bitter juice tempered with salt –
a couple of tears, the kite string
tangling itself round that phone call:
It's y' Dad, summat's up, 'e were rattlin
'is cup and 'e never does that: other folk do,
but not 'im reeling in how, after that,
one thing led to another: to me breakfasting
alone in his kitchen on scrapings
from the very last pot; to a neighbour
asking if I could let her have his empty jars –

tap tap   tap tap tap

We muffle the dead with our monuments
but still they keep up a quiet tapping on the lid
feeling for the moment *tap tap* when your focus drifts
or the moment when the axe sweetly cleaves the log
and you hear them say *Let the axe do the work*
and look down at the block *tap tap tap* and remember
how they'd adjust it: high enough not to hurt your back
low enough to catch the full speed of the blade –
this is all they are after: that you don't forget,
for when no one's left who remembers them
they can only play the crowd scenes in dreams
                                                        – who else
could they be, these strangers you're drinking tea with?
You're already late, you say, must dash else he'll worry
and you run outside and there he is, unsteady down the slope
in his shirtsleeves, away from those extras, tears spilling
down cheeks you never once saw wet in his lifetime
so you hug him, sorry you're late, but he says
This wasn't my idea, it was theirs as a young policeman
steps forward with his notebook and pencil
to detail your guilt. And how they applaud at that,
the background chorus of his fellow dead.

Old habits

Places come back to you more easily
than people – Lily's house, but not Lily –
the dim light, curtained-off stairs, black range,
chenille cloth and the damp and flying ants
and carbolic, Lily herself forever displaced
by her photo in red cardi and apron.

You can walk into the windowless scullery
behind its wood partition and green paint,
pick up the can and a bucket from the sink,
out into startling brightness beyond the trellis
and along a level path beside the drain
to the pond and the swans and The Spring Wells

without hesitation as if – like an animal
being hearthed – the first things you learn
are maps of where you belong, as if you'll
always lean over the stone slabs of a well
to dip in a bucket, rinse and fill the billy can
day after day, year after year, even

when a tap's fitted at the scullery sink,
because only The Spring Wells water tastes
right. You play the old guessing game about
where silver globules of air will wobble up next,
fill the can and pour away the perfect water
to dip and fill, dip and fill, again and again –

Love of lost things

Year after year the old-fashioned plum tree
has fruited, the weight of its yellow eggs bending
the branches until it's almost a weeping tree now.

Last year its blossoms burned in a single late frost –
but even then it made an offering, a handful
of fruits close by the trunk, their smooth gold

falling to the hand, every one valued
and warm from the sun – but I dropped one,
scuffled in long grass to find it, and found with it

a tiny feather, a jay's alula, black-barred
and so luminously blue (like lacquer over silver?)
I used to wonder at it set on my kitchen table.

Then it was gone. I searched
and kept on searching: to have lost something
come like a gift from that tree and so rare –

This year, emptying the freezer, out it flies
as blue, as beautiful as ever and yet –
yet lost, had counted more, haunted more

as still does a thin gold cross and chain
my father gave my mother before they married
or a fancy cup and saucer from my childhood mantlepiece

– losses my carelessness has cost me, rendered
so much dearer by regret and mattering far more
than ever did their simple, daily, selves.

A full renovation project with many period features

Mid-terrace. Deceptively spacious.
Your empty rooms process across my screen.
No trace now, none of the newspapers in piles,
the four year's worth of post behind the door.
They said breathing apparatus and protective clothing
were needed to clear the house:
a light had been left on, the bulb had melted;
there were unwashed pots in the sink,
untouched meals on trays, rat droppings.

The needlework would go to charity shops,
personal effects returned to family –
but what happened to your father's medals,
your brother's from the Arctic convoys?
They showed me an old photo: the thirties,
cousins at the seaside, arms linked, all three of you laughing;
I guessed you'd be the one on the right, fair-haired
and something serious about your eyes.
Or was that just your glasses?

Three bedrooms. As if looking could tell me
which was yours. Sometimes I give you
the lilac one with three picture hooks over the fireplace.
Or the yellow-painted one at the back,
sunlight and tree shadow angling across the damp.
They say you went to London at eighteen,
a bank. They say your war work was
in Churchill's bunker – though even in your nineties
Top Secret clamped your lips. So why

go back? To nurse your father, torpedoed, paralysed?
Upstairs? or did the dining-room become his world
its *Art Deco mahogany fire surround*
staring out impassive while you grieved?
Did you nurse your mother? then your sister?
How long ago did you settle yourself in that one room
where you'll gather everything you need
when you're alone and can't do stairs,
white hand-grips to steady you at every doorway.

You left no will. The law makes me
– your uncle's grand-daughter – an heir.
And here's the account of what you bequeath:
administration fees and lawyers' fees,
nursing home and undertakers' bills, a loss.
But the real loss is this: that I never knew you,
never even knew that you existed
until you became this absence in my life
which grows, the more I try to fill it in with words.

Sunday morning in the yard behind
the Wesleyan chapel

Watching Johnny work on his fifties Ford,
chrome grill, low slung and close to the road,
watching him bring back the shine, you'd say it's cars

that have changed. Sundays he's out there, the village
stops by for a shot of nostalgia: *My grandfather had one.*
It's the red front bench seat does it for me.

Changed – or is it just style: a car's still a car; homes
are still homes; cupboards, tables, changed and yet not:
the things of the body still fit the body.

Ask Johnny what's changed, he'd twist his cloth
in both hands: Johnny, he's shy, he'd not risk
the words, just point to the sign on the roadside –

FOR SALE with Permission to Demolish
lancet windows intact, worked cornerstones,
an old stillness inside starved, then forgotten.

Car

You put in petrol, and it goes and it goes.

One night it stops. The AA man says not this, not that, not that: it must be the pump. Strange, to abandon it at the roadside, to walk away.

When it comes back, you put in petrol and it goes and it goes. Over the years you buy it the usual things: batteries, wipers, tyres. A tail pipe. A front pipe. Phil tells you he's welded a steel plate underneath where your feet are, so you won't push through onto the road. A friend backs into you on a forecourt; he buys it a new wing.

You set out feeling always uncertain of arrival. You take to keeping two hours in hand for long journeys, though it never lets you down: there was only ever that one time with the pump and that was years ago. You no longer attend to its *body*.

Every day you think it a miracle to have arrived back home. One morning you notice the old car looks low at the back, as if it were weary and would not want to be roused for the road.

Against memoir

How we would run to Middlefield after they'd done,
build armchairs with the hay bales, arches, dens;
how we'd dissemble and make for forbidden places
by way of a ditch at the end of the garden –
cesspits across the aerodrome for frogspawn,
the fairground in race week, the main road;
or: celandines along the lane to St Giles like wet paint,
Life with the Lyons, woodgrain painted on brown doors,
Shippam's paste in narrow jars, collar studs, carbolic soap

– why do we do this, write so much about the past?
Why do we harry odd fragments of childhood
we can fire, briefly, with detail (real or invented), backs
turned firmly on whom we'll become, those selves
who'll slow us down, settling into our bodies
with their foibles and failing bones? Already
they're in us, trying to make themselves heard:
Learn to love us, too, they say, us and this world
you're making in which we'll have to survive.

Step theory

You thought it would happen the way
ash trees have taken over the view,
year on year higher

and more of them, until one day you turn
and notice there's no horizon
(though you like how they finger the sky)

or the way the rug by the window has faded,
strong reds shading off to grey-brown
(and that's all right too, that quiet shade)

or the way the heel of a shoe wears down
or the tines of your garden fork shine and shorten
over the years, or how a mattress hollows to fit you:

you thought the body would change
like the heart does, little by little
giving up what it loved and content with less

– though it's hard to think about age
when the sun shines. You thought changes
would be imperceptible; of no import. Well now:

Body
for Paul

A solid thing; whole.
You soon find how it bruises and bleeds.
A girl comes to class, grubby toes
poking through plaster you all write on,
draw rabbits and bows,
and it makes sense, clever really, bone
as a frame for the body, defining its form.
Then a *twang* – and you work out
stringy bits tie those bones into place.

And that's how it goes through the years:
not diagrams but breakdowns
(your own and each other's)
changing what you know of the body:
this processing plant and its filters,
a thing of tubing and piping and wires
with self-contained plumbing and pump
– some parts dispensable, some
pieced with plastic and titanium screws,

yet always some new twist, like this one:
a double-layered sac full of lubricant
whose inner parts can move against
the outer, all over and in every direction,
ingenious, extraordinary – though
not a patch on that part secreted so well
no one's uncovered it yet, the one
(even when the rest rots and cankers)
that still says *I* and *my body*.

To some moments, their own timescale

After you drove me home, my body wanted rest.
There wasn't much pain, but I trust in the body
so took to my bed. Once or twice low sun
angled round the room through the branches
but hours would pass before the shivering ceased.
Later I sat by the stove. There was no wind and no noise
just the long warmed evening, the lamplight
and the clock's slow tick louder in silence.

At the old place up north the clock had seized.
We used to set the hands to times we fancied
though our outdoor bodies went by the light.
The open-handedness of ten past ten looked good
but felt busy, catching. We favoured in-betweens:
ten to eleven, seven minutes past four.
No one ever said set it for right now,
this is the moment to hold – as I wanted to

that evening of quietness, of warmth,
flames in the stove nothing other than themselves,
gases flaring orange, waltzing round logs, and the body
without which we are nothing, at rest.

The room

Empty, apart from the curtains, yet in need
of nothing more. How can curtains fill a room?
They were to the right, drawn across the window
just short of floor-length, lifting in a silent breeze
and because they were yellow so was the room:
enlivening, serene – a room you recognised as yours
yet didn't know was there. It always was:
a room you could have danced in all along.

The back room in my first house also,
that one had yellow curtains, the window
not much over one foot wide, so only late in the day
and after the spring equinox might sunlight
reach in for an hour to gesture by the fireplace.
A junk shop desk was under stairs boxed-in
with a sliding door; the bathroom
had a sliding door, the kitchen cupboards –

touch on any one of long forgotten things
and it swings open to the rest (the fad
for purple ceilings, stick-on wood panelling)
as if the past is just a gallery of rooms:
step back in to make them *tableaux vivants*
and underneath their top coat of nostalgia
you might feel the charge they still hold on to
of loneliness, or tedium, or doubt.

Things that come in

As an old companionway ladder
from the boatbuilding years
(pitch-pine with waterproof glue
and rungs set at just the right angle)
has served in the orchard
for fruit picking and pruning
longer than it ever did on board;

as the louvre-doors from the 70's wardrobe
tacked together edgeways
with two slats removed for a pophole
made an airy, strong pen
perfect for young goslings
until they fattened and out-grew it
(dismantled now and stacked idle);

or as the cat's-eye out of its socket
found shining in the nearside verge on the moor
and re-set into an abstract painting
looms its lone signal from a certain angle,
or the dreaded side-to-middled flannelette sheets
turned up years later as good thick dusters
with neat hems and mitred corners,

so this life – more than once
irreparably broken-seeming,
its scarred parts re-assembled and extended
into something quite other: gung-ho
and ill-prepared for what's next
except knowing it won't be the same
but just might come in

the ᵒˡᵈ coat

zip hanging free at the
hem and its shoulder   seams letting in water
bot h cuffs badly frayed and one torn and a rip under the   left sleev e
worn past repair   mildewed and pockets unstitched   heavy with use:

nails	'lost'
two	blue
six inch	gloves
flatheads	penknife
galvanised	pencil stub
wire	yellow
tree-tie	label
tree-tie	black
(minus	label
spacer)	used
zip-tie	tissues
pencil stub	notebook
kitchen towel	(waterproof)
(oily)	– that day of
staples	the bird count
(three	tewits
extra large)	a hundred
stapples	and forty two
said Charlie	remember?

& a poacher's pocket I could ... nevermind I never did

And whom do you meet?
Where do you go to my lovely
When you're alone in your bed?
   – Peter Sarstedt

Emigrés. Schoolfriends
with forgotten names.
The dead of course.

Those schoolkids are older,
their adult selves:
the nine-year-old
with his brother's sweater
and a ball, a footballer;
the short one with the grin
and lopsided jaw
(it comes back to me now
he could have been a Keith)
grown into the tweed jacket
that was always in his genes
along with kindness.

Emigrés get younger, hurtle back
to their leaving age, pointing
and arranging things,
roping you in to help out
so sure of themselves:
everything they ran from,
lives they thought they'd left behind,
living lives of their own
that roll on regardless.

The same age they were
when they died, the dead
are inexplicably content.
They go about their business
much as they always did.
They have new clothes
in pale colours
and friends I've never met.
Of little interest to them now
I'm tolerated
but beside the point.
How busy they seem.

The worry hour

Already enough light to outline the landscape
like an old albumen print in soft greys,
the meadow awash with its seedheads, and pale.
White flowers in the garden like small lamps.
Everything's still; even the sleeping child's still.

This is the hour insomniacs dread –
when bodies won't heal, when memories
will fail and the whole green world you live in
falter and shrivel away ... A streak of cloud's pencilled
now on the sky, and one contrail.

Check on the child's bird-breaths, and when you look back
leaves are as ethereal as an infrared photo,
sheen on the meadow coming up yellow with buttercup.
The birch sway a little, eager for something to happen,
earth rolling east into what's next.

What can I teach the child for her unknowable future?
– light a fire with no match? find water in land drains?
How do you know? she said yesterday in the wood
when I told her the seedhead she'd picked was wild garlic
we could eat them, how do you know all these things?

A deer barks down in the wood; a blackbird is singing.
Young Martin's cockerel strangles itself on its rusty screech
exactly on time: it's four. Close the window.
I should have said, simply, it was beautiful – that sphere
of triple beads on thin stems she held up.

All summer long,

                    I slept alone in a high room
with a low window that gave on to the valley
from a new angle. Without books
I would lie watching dusk gather above the river
and seep upwards through the Old Wood
until landscape massed black against midnight sky.

An owl would settle above the open window
between the evening's preparations
and the business of the night and shriek
– not once her full *keee-wik*, only an insistent
wik wik wik. Most nights two males called back
hoo hoooo from the Old Wood; once, three.

What you write about your life displaces
remembering: instead of memory's
murky mutability, the conviction
of the printed word. So let me overwrite
that time with a bite – hard – from a mole,
or with my hands cupped round a pipistrelle

(inexplicable refugee from daylight's brilliance
splayed on the kitchen floor) as I carried its fury
to a secret darkness in a garden corner,
its chatter of growls and barks and protests
testing the crevices between my fingers.
As for the rest of that summer,
                              let it go.

Sleeping out

No wind in the pines –
I didn't believe the forecast
yet pulled my bivvy bag
part-way under the awning
where I could still see the stars.

When I woke, it had snowed
a light coverlet on me; more
– say two inches – on the ground
and melting already
so the tracks of a creature

which had stalked round
my unknowing body
were hard to decipher,
their indents collapsing:
four-toed I thought –

a fox's most likely
or were the prints wider,
the tread of a wildcat?
Some moist muzzle
had leaned close by my head

breathing my breath
and eavesdropping dreams
while taking my measure
along and back then around
– much the same as the way

I might sniff at a spraint
or track deer slots
to a lair, as if I might
bed down too, try out
how the world feels from there.

As if just by listening

January first-quarter moon
birch-gleam lightly chalked on the night
and a darkness   hunched   close by the trunk

evening after evening   called out
to the dark and cold   to listen
(sometimes supper half-eaten on the table)

closing the door no matter how quietly
– if they can hear a mouse under thick frozen snow –
every movement of mine   loud on their map

as if just by listening
understanding   might fall to the ear
with the grace of a language

later   even in sleep   tensed
for the next hoot
a not-quite-woken awareness   drawn

to the edge of the Old Wood downhill
their calls in dream   all easy exchange –
Yes, yes! I reply, *as soon as I can*

I know a man bought laboratory mice
that last hard winter we had   laid out
a handful along a branch at last light

near where owls roosted   then a dozen
when the freeze deepened to minus 9
he said there were three   he knew by their voices

Hymenoscyphus fraxineus

comes   creeping
comes on the quiet   inconspicuous
comes crabwise comes
canny   biding its time
          one eye on the weather
covers its tracks
skulks

eructs
encroaches   catches
you unaware
colonises
          covert but cocksure
until cracks appear
                    gape and
conquer

catastrophe you say
human
       and culpable
you
    with your commerce
cankers   carted
incognito

Wind and woods

gusts battering the Little Wood in full leaf
heave sway and rollback   heave sway roll back

yet inside it's quiet   mosses yielding to the foot
leaf litter, mole workings, sweet smells of decay
                    (rot, fungus and toadstool)
wind roar smoothed by the canopy
to a sound like little waves hissing over sand

quieter still late October after sharp frost
hazel leaves yellow against blue sky
and you yourself the only wind –
make the smallest perturbation of the air
and they let go all at once puttering to the ground
(somewhere behind you another leaf fall
startles in the silence)

millions over the years and more millions

one   settling furtive on the woodland floor
leaflets crumbling to leafmould, stalk
black and stiff – still there after rains, after snow
after more rains, after windflowers and grasses
here and there bluebells – you'd not notice it come June
its length pimpled with tiny white specks
swelling a little   you'd notice
nothing of this   membranes rupturing

and the millions more millions

of spores surfing the breeze   to settle
and fail – most falling on grass some falling on tarmac
some on roofs on brambles onto oak leaves

and some on top of a passing wagon
which reverses down a track then turns across the wind
so they're lifted up and off again   free
to re-settle their invisible deadliness
on the clean new leaves of a sapling ash –
a self-seeded adventurer
which had been   heading for the sky

One place

When you've lived all your adult life in one place,
you fell trees. You planted them too close
or blocked the view or some sickened. Like us

they go for height till they're twenty, then thicken. That's true
of the ash and the birch, but not oak: they're
stunted. You never know how an oak will shape up.

You drop logs in the stove without regret, though
they're recognisable still – that birch by the kitchen,
even a length of eucalypt from the garden.

I'm still planting trees, though I know I'll not see
how they'll grow and can't even imagine
the shapes they might make against winter sky.

Downspouts are busy, full of short vowels.
We're burying my neighbour tomorrow, my birthday.
Ice is forecast, then snow. We'll see.

When you've lived in one place so long, there's someone
you know in every row. The way it's worked out,
my friends are at the far side, by the wall.

The hearse has to go the long way, over the moor.
It's nearer on foot, though it still feels removed from the world,
the church in its hollow, the stone walls.

When you've lived your life in one parish
and gather with neighbours for a burial,
you think the same thoughts as everyone else:
is that Tom? – still handsome, though that coat's
tight on the shoulders. We polish our glasses,
hold hymn sheets out at arm's length.
George is completely white now. Ruby is too.
One of us will be the next: what someone remembers
we said one time passed round and repeated.
Then all of us will be stories, just stories, no names.

✳

A perfect fan preserved in the snow
where a pheasant pressed down its spread tail
for take-off. The grave's right next to the footpath.

When you've lived most of your life with the same people
sharing your weather and power cuts and floods,
they start to pass on their tales that keep mortality at bay.
You're supposed to remember the names
though even the teller forgets: who was it had the top field
above the graveyard in those days, Billy Morphet?
or his brother? anyway, he and the gravedigger
were having a smoke, the two of them up by the wall,
when Jimmy Read comes along. He doesn't let on:
he gets in the hole and lies down and keeps quiet
– just think on it, laid there, listening out –
the gravedigger nearly falls in on top with the shock.

Mind you, he said after, six foot ... it's a long way down.

✳

When you know a place lifelong, you've no need of maps;
every name has its shapes and its feel underfoot:
Helks, Jacksons Pasture, Perry Moor – even the fields
have names: Robins Close, Parrocks Meadow.

But who was Jackson? who was Robin? – you know nothing
of them, the datestones they set over their doorways
outlasting them as they knew they would –
but not calling them up. Just the year, just initials.

The one great oak at the top of the Old Wood
above the river – who planted that? Or was it a jay?
Since Ken laid the roadside hedge for me last year,
passers-by can see the trees I planted twenty years ago

as if they're new and sudden. I've heard it called Ken's Wood
– not Jane's. They look lovely from the road,
strong trunks and straight and more beyond on rising ground.
I scattered foxglove seeds among them, and ramsons too.

November mood music

The cloudless afternoon starts to fade.
A short pink contrail from over the pole
crawls across the sky to this city or that.
Nothing else moves.

Computer models struggle.
Forecasts are wrong: windless so long
leaves fell straight down, settled
in perfect circles round the trunks.

The magnetic north pole's lurched east.
The planet wobbles closer to drop-off.
I rake up yellow roundels under the hazel,
their fine velvet nap still damp. How to bear

the news? Easier when there were gods
and afterlives. The gold leaves top off the heap
already higher than me: next year's leafmould
for next year's planting – faith of some sort.

Acknowledgements and notes

Thanks are due to the editors of publications in which some of these poems first appeared: *Magma, Strix, The Clearing, The Compass, The Moth, The North, The Scores; Solstice* (ed. S. Hymas & R. Bilkau, Beautiful Dragons Press, 2012), *The Tower of Babel* (ed. R. Loydell, Like This Press, 2013).

'One Place' won the 2011 Strokestown International Poetry Competition; 'Holy Detritus' was commissioned for an exhibition of the same name by St Oswald's Church, Grasmere 2013; '3am' was commissioned by Magdalene College, Cambridge for their Festival of Sound and Place 2015.

'*Hymenoscyphus fraxineus*' (and the poem which follows it) questions received wisdom that these fungus spores, which cause ash die-back disease, blew across the English Channel from the continent against our prevailing winds. Disease distribution maps show it started near to and spread out from the south east ports. Co-incidentally, *Hedges* – the subject of 'Elegy for a book' – shows the arrival of Dutch elm disease in the 1970s was 'related to port areas', its authors concluding 'There seems to be a danger that other tree diseases ... could be introduced in the same way'.